An Introduction to Habit Stacking - How to Change Your Life Meaningfully

100 Essential Life Changes

Steven Tyler

Copyright 2018 by Samantha Taylor - All rights reserved

determine what state and/or local laws or regulations may apply to the user's particular business.

The purchaser or reader of this publication assumes responsibility for the use of these materials and information. Adherence to all applicable laws and regulations, federal, state, and local, governing professional licensing, business practices, advertising, and all other aspects of doing business in the United States or any other jurisdiction is the sole responsibility of the purchaser or reader.

The author and Publisher assume no responsibility or liability whatsoever on the behalf of any purchaser or reader of these materials for injury due to use of any of the methods contained herein. Any perceived slights of specific people or organizations are unintentional.

Table of Contents

Introduction: Are You Looking For A Way to Lead a Better Life?

Are you one of those people who feel that they can get more out of life but are unable to do so? Do you feel that you can never make a lasting change in your life? Do you feel that you always make an optimistic start to change your life but a week later go back to your old ways? What if we were to tell you that there is a easy way to get the life you want. The secret in making a permanent change in life is making lots of tiny changes which lead to bigger changes.

Want to Get Healthier?

Are you one of those people who want to fit more exercise into your day to lead a healthier life? Are you also one of those people who have made resolutions about the exercise you should be doing on a daily basis? Have you made numerous starts to becoming healthier? Do you fail to stick to your new habit after the first few days? The important thing to remember is not to get disheartened if you have a setback - there are millions of people in the same boat and all of them wonder how to stick to new goals. The good thing is that we now have a solution at hand to help you attain your goal.

Want to Lose Weight?

Are you one of those people who have wanted to lose weight? If you find yourself in this particular predicament then you will find it heartening to know that you aren't the only one facing this problem. If you have made new year resolutions to lose weight but after January find yourself giving up on the resolutions then you are like the most of us. However, all this can change with the new method we will introduce in this book.

Looking to Increase Productivity at Work?

Do you feel that you aren't your productive and creative best at work? Do you feel that you are held back or wasting time on pointless tasks at work? Do you find yourself surfing online for up to an hour at a time? Don't beat yourself up about this. This is exactly the dilemma a lot of professionals face in their day-to-day lives and wonder what they can do about it. All is not lost, by taking small bite-sized steps you can now make the changes required for you to be more productive at work.

Figuring Out How to Save More Money?

Are you one of those people who realize the importance of saving money and looking at your finances carefully? We all know it's important to save money for a rainy day. We all know we need to put a little money on the side for an emergency. However, in our daily lives we struggle to save due to lack of planning, wastage of money, not having time, or lacking foresight to find the best deals available for our money, utility bills, groceries bills and general shopping. We can provide you some comfort by telling you that you can start saving effectively right away.

Need to Sort Out Relationship Woes?

Do you feel you are in a rut in terms of your relationship with your girlfriend? Do you feel that you could do better by your family? Do you feel that you could be a better friend but haven't been able to show your friendship credentials lately? Do you feel that you could be a better acquaintance, neighbour, or work colleague? Do you think you are generally letting your personal or professional relationships suffer? This is a common issue people face in their daily lives. We are so busy with work and other issues that we often don't have time for the people in our lives. The technique we will introduce in this book will help make time for people in your lives.

Looking to Declutter Your Life?

Are you one of those people who are looking to organize their life in physical, mental and emotional terms? Do you want all the clutter, fluff and mess present in your home and life to get cleared away but don't know how to make a start? Do you want things in your emotional, mental and physical universe to be tidy and organized? Perhaps you are the ideal candidate for reading this book. We can help you declutter your home, office and life.

Trying to Figure Out Your Spirituality?

Are you one of those people who are busy all the time, achieved a lot in life but still feel strangely empty? Do you always feel as if you are lost? Do you feel as if you are searching for something but aren't exactly sure what it is? Do you feel that you need a bit of spirituality in your life in order to see the light so to speak? Well, the technique we are going to introduce will allow you to get time to figure out all the spiritual aspects of your life no matter how busy or tired you are.

Habit Stacking

The rather unique idea that we will be introducing and discussing with our readers in this book is known as habit stacking. Habit stacking is a unique, easy to understand, easy to follow idea which guarantees results. We are now going to discuss this idea in detail in part I of our book.

PART I: HABIT STACKING - AN ANSWER TO A LOT OF YOUR PROBLEMS

Chapter 1: What is Habit Stacking?

Now, we are going to introduce the solution to a lot of your problems in ten easy steps through a technique called habit stacking. You are probably wondering what exactly is habit stacking? Habit stacking is a stupidly simple process where you take small individual actions and stack them together to work effectively towards a larger habit change. Instead of considering these small individual actions as discrete tasks you need to think of them as one habit stack or small parts of the whole.

This chapter will show you how easy, time saving and effective habit stacking can be if you want to take on new habits and ditch some old ones. The key thing to remember is that patience, small steps and consistency will get you where you want to be. Small achievable goals need to be set and your memory muscle needs to get use to completing tasks and feeling rewarded. Then you can stack up further and achieve bigger victories and goals.

Step 1: Spend a Few Minutes Setting New Habits

Starting on a journey to set new habits and work towards the habit you want is simple and only take a couple of minutes each day. You might think that a couple of minutes is a bit of a joke but it's a small manageable start to making sure you correct yourself. The important thing to remember when you want to set new habits start small and aim big. If you want to start exercising begin with five minutes each day. If you want to start writing spend five minutes each day writing a paragraph or two. If you want to declutter your home why not set the timer for five minutes and then clean up as much as you can. If you want to be in touch with your family or friends then why not spend five minute giving a family member or friend a call everyday.

Step 2: Celebrate Small Victories

It is important to celebrate small victories as this provides us with the momentum to keep going for bigger goals. Start writing a paragraph a day, drinking eight glasses of water, completing a few minutes of yoga every day, or spending a couple of minutes cleaning - all small goals but there is a purpose to these small victories. These small changes will lead to other small changes which will lead to more significant changes in your life. So celebrating your small daily victories is very important for changing your life overall.

Step 3: Pick a Time and Location

When you are looking to set new habits it's important to pick a certain time and location to carry out your goals. So if you want to exercise why not get up first thing in the morning, go to the living room and practice yoga. If you want to be healthy why not get up in the morning and drink two glasses of water in the kitchen. If you want to write why not find some time in the evening after dinner and spend 5 minutes writing. It's important to get into a new habit or set of habits with the help of a time schedule and location that you pick for yourself.

Step 4: Set Up a Trigger for Your New Habit

One of the things you can do to make your new habit easier to follow is set up a trigger. This trigger can be internal or external - what ever is easier to follow. Say, your goal is to have five minutes of exercise each day, then why not set an alarm for 7.00 am each day to remind you to exercise each day. If you want to drink two glasses of water at the start of your day why not keep a water bottle on your bedside table so its the first thing you see in the morning. If you want to floss after brushing your teeth then why not keep the floss next to your tooth brush. If you would like to check your emails then set a remainder for 5 minutes first thing in the morning when you check your emails.

Step 5: Create a Check List

Another way to make sure that you are able to follow through with your new habit is through creating a checklist. Say you would like to drink 8 glasses of water a why not set up a small checklist to make sure you stay on track. If you need to take vitamins or a snack at a certain time of the day why not give yourself an electronic reminder. If you want to squeeze in 15 minutes of yoga everyday during the week why not set up a weekly calendar.

Step 6: Hold Yourself Accountable

One of the things to help you make sure you are able to attain your small goals is the ability to hold yourself accountable. Often when you set goals for yourself you are not doing much to attain them because you aren't held accountable.

Sometimes it just isn't enough to make personal goals - perhaps you should join a group with similar goals and share your progress with them, perhaps you should post your goals on social media or perhaps you should ask your family and friends to be your support network.

Step 7: Reward Yourself

If you manage to complete your tasks properly at the end of the day you can reward yourself with a small treat. A small treat could be half an hour of quiet time, watching your favourite show, having a small glass of wine, having a soak in the bath, having a healthy snack, listening to your favourite songs or just having 'me' time any way you like. However, the rewards should be carefully chosen and shouldn't reinforce any negative habits.

Step 8: Rewind and Play

Another important thing to remember is that repetition is the key to success in terms of habit stacking. You need to exercise, write a paragraph, paint, meditate or de-clutter your home on a daily basis in small manageable chunks.   Habits are made with practice and effort and you need to make the effort every single day.

Step 9: Expect Setbacks and Learn to Move on

Even with the best of intentions there will be days where you can't manage to carry out your planned habits. If it's the occasional set back then there is no need to worry you just need to learn from your mistakes and move on. There may be certain negative triggers which give you these set backs or there might be an emergency or sickness which prevents you from doing so.

Step 10: Scale up Your Stack

It's important to figure out at what point you have got into the habit of doing something such as exercise, eating healthy, reading, writing, meditating or doing yoga. If you feel that you are comfortably in the habit of doing something then why not scale up. Why not go from exercising for five minutes to ten minutes, why not do a 15 minute session of yoga each day, why not write two instead of one paragraph, how about meditating for ten minutes.

Note: One Habit at a Time.

If you are trying to overhaul your lifestyle then it's important to remember that habit stacking works well if you try and change one habit at a time. Once you feel you have settled into one good habit properly then it's time for start another habit stacking for another new habit. Remember change comes in small achievable amounts not large random chunks.

Chapter 2: The Philosophy Behind Habit Stacking

We have just discussed the main steps behind the process of habit stacking and now we are going to look at the philosophy behind this system of inculcating good habits and doing away with procrastination. The term 'habit stacking' was established by author S.J Scott. His book *Habit Stacking: 97 Small Life Changes That Take Five Minutes or Less* states that you can, "build routines around habits that don't require effort" because "small wins build momentum because they're easy to remember and complete."

1. New Habits a Part of Your Existing Routine

Now we all have a to-do-list that we never really get around to completing. One of the main reasons for this is we are creatures of set habit. We tend to get fixed in a rut just doing the same things again and again. However, through adding small actions to an already established routine we can take up new habits. Say you always feel like taking up meditation but never really find the time to do it. You picture yourself having a free half an hour to meditate. However, in reality you can hardly ever fit in such a long period of time for meditation. If you want to pick up something new why not fit in five or ten minutes of meditation immediately after you walk up in the morning. Why not anchor your meditation to the start of your new day. The five or ten minutes you spend in bed walking up can be spent focusing on meditation which will clear your mind up.

2. Anchoring Habits with Triggers

The problem with forming new habits is that you might forget to make those new things a part of your day. However, what if you used the things that were already a part of your daily routine to remind you of the things that you should be doing. For example, perhaps you want to floss your teeth everyday but keep forgetting to take the floss out. Why not put the floss next to your tooth brush so that whenever you brush you can remember to floss. Or if you want to moisturize your face before going to bed put night face cream next to your bed side table. Perhaps, you want to read a chapter of a book each day, well put the book in your bag and take it out whenever you are sitting on the tube on your way to work or on your way home.

3. Setting Bite Sized Chunks

Another important aspect behind the philosophy of habit stacking is keeping new habits or behaviour patterns restricted to bite-sized chunks. We would love to exercise for half an hour everyday but we know in reality we would struggle. So how about breaking up 30 minutes into three 10 minute intense exercise periods and carrying out a ten minute period of exercise before every main meal you eat in a day. Breaking goals into manageable bite sized goals will make them more attainable. Perhaps you want to learn a language and can't find a sold 1 hour to spend time picking up new language skills. Why not spread your learn through out the day - every time you have a coffee break spend 5-10 minutes looking through your language book or notes. That way you can regularly brush up on your language skills.

4. Strengthening Those Synapses in Your Mind

There is a biological phenomenon that takes place as we age known as synaptic pruning. Synapses are the branch looking connections between the neurons in your brain. The basic idea is that your brain prunes away connections between neurons that don't get used and builds up connections in locations where neurons get used more frequently.

Say you have enjoyed doing crossword puzzles given in your paper every morning at the breakfast table. Because you have been doing these puzzle every morning, your brain strengthens the synapses and strengthens your ability to figure out crossword puzzles. The more you practice cross word puzzles the stronger your synapse connections become and the more efficient you get at doing cross world puzzles. However, if you never do crossword puzzles your brain will prune away the synapses for this skill and strengthen synapse connections for other life skills.

5. Making a List of Daily Tasks

To be successful at habit stacking you need to have a clear idea of the activities you carry out in the course of an ordinary day. Why not sit down with a pen and paper and start thinking what you do through out your day from the point that you get up till the point you hit the sack. Once you have figured out and written down all the activities you do you can start making a list of things you would like to add into your existing day.

The best thing about habit stacking is that you make use of your existing daily routine so that you don't have to make big changes in your existing routine you only have to make small additions to your existing routine.

6. Making a List of Things you Would Like to do

The real fun starts with the second list - we would like you to sit down with a pen and another sheet of paper. We would now like you to write down what you would like to achieve on a daily basis. We would like you to put in some real thought into this as it will shape how your day goes. Make a list of things that you can do on a daily basis - exercise, meditation, writing, reading, working more, working less, spending more time with your family.

7. Practice, Practice and Practice

Once you have the list of your daily routine and a list of things you want to incorporate into your daily routine by tagging them to a series of internal and external triggers, it is necessary to put things through practice. It takes between 21 and 45 days to get used to new habits; so go ahead practice, practice and practice.

Chapter 3: Ground Rules For Habit Stacking

Chapter 3 looks at the ground rules for habit stacking which you need to remember when you set up a routine of good and positive habits. We are now laying down eight simple rules to help you with your process of habit stacking. We feel these eight points will help remind you what is important when setting up a positive routine. You can keep these rules in front of you as you plan your habit stacking process through the course of the day.

Rule 1. Each Habit Should Take no More Than 5 minutes.

The first rule to ensure any new habit you want to incorporate into your day is the new habit should be no more than five minutes in length. Now five minutes may not seem very much to you but when inculcating a new habit it's important to keep things short and sweet. Starting off small and simple ensures that you find the tasks easy and are more likely to inculcate them into your daily routine. The main thing to remember is that starting out small you can build up something worthwhile.

Rule 2. It's A Complete Habit

It is important to plan something which takes no more than five minutes and is also a complete action. You need to have a think about this carefully to ensure that in five minutes you can carry out a complete habit. This means that you can't keep making it any harder than it is. A complete task could be drinking a glass of water when you wake up first thing in the morning. It could be a five minute meditation exercise. It may be eating fruit before your breakfast in the morning. It could be saying a gratitude prayer after completing each meal. It may be flossing after you have brushed your teeth. Moisturizing or putting sun block cream on before you go out of the door is another complete task. It could be a journal looking at how your day went.

Rule 3. It Improves Your Life

The whole point of habit stacking is it gets to change your life in a positive way. So you need to have a bit of reflection about how the habits you are incorporating will help improve your life for the better. For example drinking water, eating healthy, taking vitamins, doing exercise and practicing mediation all improve your life. However, there are certain habits which might not be positive at all such as spending more time on social media, spending more time on the phone, spending time looking through your emails. Would you want to incorporate these activities into your daily life.

Rule 4. It's Simple To Complete

Another thing you need to remember is that any task you take up in your five minutes needs to be simple to complete. The tasks should be short, simple and seamlessly fit into your normal daily routine. Given that your tasks are short, they probably aren't too rigorous - this way you can see quick and visible changes and improvements. So start with simple tasks which make a big positive difference in your life and bring in an improved form of life for you.

Rule 5. The Routine Should Take No More Than 30 Minutes.

When you make a list of things you would like to incorporate in your daily routine make sure there aren't more than five or six new things you initially incorporate. This is to ensure that you don't get overwhelmed by the new routine you set up for yourself. In the beginning start out simple with a few positive or healthy changes in your daily routine. Perhaps, you want to drink a glass of water when you wake up, take a vitamin before breakfast, do a five minute meditation practice, or remember to put on that sunscreen before you head out for the day. If these are the five things you initially want to include then that is all you should practice initially.

Rule 6. Your Routine Should Follow A Logical Process.

Another thing which you need to keep in mind is your new habits should follow a logical process. You need to have a look at the tasks or habits you want to include in your day: For example you need to drink a glass or two of water and mediate as soon as you get up, take your vitamin and eat fruit before cooking yourself breakfast and you need to remember to put on the sunscreen before you get out of the door. You need to prioritize your tasks in terms of the rooms you carry them out in. You can drink a glass or water and mediate in your bedroom first thing in the morning. You can eat your vitamin and a fruit in the kitchen. Finally, you can put on sunscreen in the hallway before leaving. So you need to remember to complete all the tasks you have set for one room before moving into the next room.

Rule 7. It Follows a Checklist.

It will help if you follow a checklist that you have made of your routine with the new habits incorporated. Perhaps you can take a peak at this checklist through out the day and see whether you are going according to what you planned. This may sound tedious and a bit of an over kill but believe me it will help you during the first few weeks to keep on track and inculcate the new routine in to your life. The important thing initially is to get into the flow of doing things. Once you have gotten yourself in the groove of doing things a little differently you can let go of the check list.

Rule 8. It fits your life.

The final rule is a stupid but necessary one - you need to make sure that the way you have planned your habit stacking is beneficial to you or something that you will be able to follow through. Say you would like to practice yoga and meditation but you know you can't do it first thing in the morning as you aren't exactly an early bird - why not carry out these activities later on in the day perhaps in the afternoon or the evening.

Chapter 4: How to Set SMART Goals?

Chapter 4 looks at how you can go about setting the right type of goals when habit stacking. In this chapter we are going to teach you how to set some smart goals. You may have heard of SMART goals before, a lot of people use this concept to set SMART personal and professional goals in their day-to-day lives. This is an incredibly helpful and powerful concept when we are making goals for the new year, or to set new habit, or when we generally want to make our life go in another direction.

When we think of setting goals, it's a good idea to try and break them down into manageable portions - in case of habit stacking it's bite-sized goals that we are looking for. We often struggle because we might not be making the sort of goals that we have the motivation, will, passion to achieve. To set up the right type of goals we are going to introduce you to the concept of SMART goals.

We first begin by defining what exactly SMART means, SMART stands for:

- **S** = Specific (it can also stand for Strategic)

- **M** = Measurable (it can also stand for Motivation

- **A** = Assignable (it can be used to represent Agreed, attainable, action-oriented, ambitious, aligned with corporate goals,

- **R** = Relevant (it can also stand for Realistic, resourced, reasonable, realistic and resourced and results-based)

- **T** = Time related (T can also be used for trackable, time-based, time limited, time/cost limited, timely, time-sensitive, time-frame and testable

Perhaps you can write what SMART stands for on a card and then look at your stated goal in terms of the SMART goal concept. This way you might have to put in a bit more work to get your goals sorted, defined and broken into bite sized milestones but in the long run it will be worth the effort. At least you will think of your goals in terms of specific, measurable, assignable, relevant and time related goals. There will be some clear and tangible milestones set for each goal which means you have more of a chance of meeting your goal.

We are now going to present a couple of examples keeping in mind the SMART goal concept.

Let's come back to the goal of losing weight during the course of this year. We can now have a think about it in terms of the SMART goal concept. Your specific goal could be losing enough weight to allow your BMI to be healthy. To make this goal measurable you might decide you need to lose 20 pounds. You could agree to lose it through a change in diet and through increase in exercise. What would make this goal realistic is losing about 1-2 pounds each month. You could also make this goal time specified by stating that it should take a year to lose 20 pounds. This way you could make sure that you have a SMART goal in terms of weight loss.

Say you have a New Year goal of leading a healthier life and wonder how you want to tailor it in accordance to SMART goals concept. You could set a specific target of getting some exercise on a daily basis in order to have a healthier, happier and active life. If you want a measurable factor to your goal you can state that you want to get at least 30 minutes of physical exercise each day. You could do this at home, outside in your neighborhood or even in the local gym. You want to start by any realistic form of activity such as taking a walk around your local neighbourhood. Time-related goal of following 30 minutes of exercise each day across the whole year.

Perhaps, you want to follow through with the goal of saving more in the year so you can put it away for a rainy day fund or think about putting down a deposit for a home. Lets see how you can use the SMART goal concept to help you set up your goals. When you think about the specific goal then perhaps you can say that you want to save rather than spend all your income in a year. In terms of measurable goals you could set your goal at say 6,000 dollars. You can make this attainable through saving 500 dollars a month or 125 dollars a week through carefully budgeting your income. Your time related goal could be for the course of a year and then you could re-evaluate your goal.

Another way the SMART goals concept can be used is to help you set goals for your spirituality. Why not sit down and think about how you want to have a think in terms of your spirituality. Think about what exactly you want in your life in terms of spirituality, how you would like to practice or show your spirituality. How long would you like to spend practicing your spirituality each day? Perhaps you can spend 5 minutes each day practicing or thinking about your spirituality. You could track your spiritual journey through keeping a diary or journal.

As can be seen by the above four examples SMART goals are clearer, conciser, specific and more to the point than your normal resolutions and goal setting. It also gives you a way of thinking about your goals constructively by looking at all the different factors involved in your goal-making. The more you think about, understand, and strive for these goals the more likely you are to achieve these goals.

Why not jot down what SMART stands for and get on with making sure your goals are SMART goals. If you can't make a SMART goal out of what you want in life then don't opt for this particular goal. Leave it aside and work on those that you can make SMART.

PART II: HOW TO USE HABIT STACKING TO CREATE THE LIFE YOU WANT

Chapter 5. Health Related Habit Stacking

Chapter 5 takes a look at how you can make your lives healthier by attempting small tweaks to your daily routine. We always make big plans about hitting the gym daily, practicing meditation, or only eating organic and healthy food. More often than not all this planning leads to nothing being practically achieved. The main reason for this is we set ourselves up for failure - we set extremely high, unattainable, perfect-looking goals. Understandably, we find these goals daunting and shy away from doing anything practically. What we don't realize is sometimes it is the short and sweet that works for us. Keeping things simple and small is the trick.

Some Popular Health Aims

Some of the common health aims people would like to see themselves achieve are listed below. Health aims are a combination of physical, mental and   emotional well-being goals. We will now see how we can try and fit as many of them as possible in our daily lives:

Physical Well Being

- Drink 8 glasses of water prescribed per day.

- Eat three balanced and healthy meals a day.

- Take five helpings of fruit or vegetables a day.

- Take relevant health supplements to keep your body and mind healthy.

- Take medicines you need to manage existing health conditions.

- Sit less & move more as 30 minutes of activity are required daily.

- Get the recommended 6-8 hours of sufficient sleep.

Mental Well Being

- De-stress as it's beneficial for your physical and mental health.

- Practice meditation to relax the mind.

- Practice mindfulness to think with greater clarity.

- Have faith or spirituality as it helps with the tough times.

- Keep working as it keeps your mind active and body alert.

- Learn new things to keep your mind alert and flexible.

- Venture out of your comfort zone and try new things.

Emotional Well Being

- Maintain a regular routine which keeps you mentally & emotionally alert.

- Be social and meet family and friends for your emotional well-being.

- Be kind towards yourself and others.

- Remain positive and sunny in your outlook.

- Be conscientious about important life decisions.

- Show gratitude for all that you have been blessed with.

- Reflect on your life to see how you can improve it and what lessons are learned.

Achieving These Health Aims

We have listed 21 common health aims which a lot of people would like to achieve. You could try incorporating a mixture of health aims from across the categories or tackle one category at a time. For the purpose of this chapter we will tackle one category at a time. We mentioned in chapter 3 discussing rules for habit stacking that it's necessary in the beginning to ensure that you spend no more than half an hour on the additions you add to your daily routine. Six or seven points will equate to half an hour - you might think that these changes amount to nothing but these small steps have the ability to make big changes in your life.

Physical Well-Being

If you are one of those people aiming for physical well-being but don't quite know how to fit some of the aims listed above into your daily routine why not try the following: Set your alarm clock half an hour earlier than your normal waking time and then do a few things while still in bed. You can get up with the sound of your alarm clock and drink that glass of water you are always meaning . You can also fit in five minutes of yoga or light exercise - these activities are done in the comfort of your bedroom without you starting your day. You can also try and figure out whether the medicine you have to take or the vitamin supplements you want to take can also be kept in your bedroom. All four of these activities will not take more than 10 minutes at the start of your day and you have made a cracking start to your day.

You can now have a think about what you can get done in the kitchen - you could eat some fruit and make a fiber rich breakfast which ensures you start the day on a healthy note. After breakfast you can have a think about the things you need to do in the bathroom - shower, brush your teeth, floss your teeth and applying moisturizer or sun block cream. Now all these extra things you have tagged onto your daily routine will take no more than 20 extra minutes. The beauty of it is you will still feel as if you are following your original daily routine.

We have shown below in step form how you can sneak these new habits into your daily routine.

Step 1: Wake Up

Step 2: Drink water

Step 3: Five minutes of exercise

Step 4: Take your vitamin

Step 5: Eat a fruit

Step 6:Prepare breakfast

Step 7: Have a shower

Step 8: Brush your teeth

Step 9: Floss your teeth

Step 10: Get dressed

Step 11: Apply moistur

Mental Well-Being

We often concentrate on aspects of our physical well-being such as losing weight, making sure we exercise enough, eating healthy food and drinking enough water. However, we tend to forget that the same type of effort and vigilance needs to be made for our mental well-being. We are now going to take a look at how we can take care of our mental health by adding small steps to our daily routine.

A lot of the things we feel we should devote a lot of time to we tend to keep putting off because we are daunted by the effort they will take. However, the key to our success is taking small baby steps to look after ourselves and mentally checking in with ourselves on a regular basis. Some of the things we assume will take half an hour can be done by devoting five minutes to them each day.

When you wake up in the morning why not devote five minutes for meditation followed by five minutes of prayer or any other spiritual ritual you would like to do. This helps pay attention to your mental state and needs for the day. Two other things that you can try in bite sized chunks on a daily basis is learning or trying something new such as learning a language, playing a piece of music or trying to master a new dance step. Lastly, to keep yourself mentally alert try to spend five-ten minutes doing something or trying to master something you are not comfortable with. All of these things will keep you on your toe and mentally alert and fresh. We are building up our morning schedule by tending to your physical and mental health needs.

Step 1: Wake up

Step 2: Waking up prayer

Step 3: Five minutes of meditation

Step 4: Glass of water

Step 5: Five minutes of exercise

Step 6: Taking your vitamin

Step 7: Eating a piece of fruit

Step 8: Preparing a health breakfast

Step 9: Reading something new

Step 10: Have a shower

Step 11: Brush teeth

Step 12: Floss

Step 13: Get dressed

Step 14: Moisturize

Emotional Well-Being

The third type of well-being you should keep in touch with is your emotional well-being. Our emotions are one thing that we haven't been taught to keep in touch with and aren't encouraged to discuss openly. A lot of us don't really look inwards to see how we are feeling. Emotional health is an important facet of our personality and we need to put in just as much work to keep ourselves healthy in this area as we do for our physical and mental health.

The habits listed under the emotional well-being section may look like a lot of work but these are bite-sized tasks which don't have to take too much time. Try waking up in the morning and spending five minutes saying something optimistic and positive to yourself as this will start your day on a good note. Perhaps try writing in your journal for five minutes without thinking too much about the day ahead while still in bed.Why not say a prayer of gratitude every time you sit down to have a meal. If you have enough time at breakfast why not pick up a book or a newspaper and read something you enjoy.

The steps we have provided below now incorporate tasks which help improve your physical, mental and emotional health.

Step 1: Wake up

Step 2: Waking up prayer

Step 3: Recite a positive mantra

Step 4: Write in a personal diary

Step 5: Five minutes of meditation

Step 6: Glass of water

Step 7: Five minutes of exercise

Step 8: Taking your vitamin

Step 9: Eating a piece of fruit

Step 10: Preparing a health breakfast

Step 11: Saying a gratitude prayer

Step 12: Reading something new

Step 13: Have a shower

Step 14: Brush
teeth

Step 15: Floss

Step 16: Get
dressed

Step 17:
Moisturize

Step 18: Spent
five minutes
visualizing a
good day

Chapter 6. Career Related Habit Stacking

We all want a really productive, creative and high flying career but in reality we find ourselves struggling with mundane tasks we face on a daily basis and a mountain of never-ending work. We often find ourselves derailed from absolutely key tasks by dozens of small mindless tasks which have no productivity value in our career. Sometimes we might find that we are unable to address the really important issues at hand or figure out a way to further our career. In this chapter we are going to figure out how to habit stack effectively at work.

Some Popular Career Aims

Some of the top work related aims most people would like to make sure come their way are:

- Improvement in work indicators that show you are more productive.

- Getting a professional degree as it opens up more work opportunities.

- Finding flexible work which helps ensure a work life balance.

- Getting a promotion.

- Changing jobs so you can work where you want.

- Starting your own business so you can do what you love.

- Being an expert in your field so that you creative a niche for yourself.

- Being in an management position.

- Being more efficient at work.

- Being more productive at work.

- Being able to get personal development chances.

- Improve communication skills.

- Improve presentation skills.

- Improve networking skills.

- Improving your work life balance.

You might ask yourself how an earth do you use habit stacking to achieve some of the above popular work-related claims. Well we use habit stacking for furthering our career in the same way as we use habit stacking in working to improve our health. We take small, bite-sized, SMART goals and try to work new habits almost seamlessly into our daily routine.

Habit Stacking For Your Career

Suppose we want to start using the habit stacking process to help us improve and further our career aspirations. We use the same concepts: we use an internal or external tag to which we attach new habits. We basically concentrate on how we can use the same daily routine to fit in things which are beneficial for our career.

Helping your career along on a daily basis can start from the night before - when during the evening when you have your glass of wine after a meal you sit down and have a rummage through your mind about the things you need to do the following day. What are some of the things you will need to think about tomorrow at work. Is there anything you can do the evening before to help your day go smoothly? Perhaps a five to ten minute read through your emails. Perhaps sorting out your electronic schedule or your diary. Perhaps jotting down the things you need to get out of the door tomorrow before end of play.

A good way to start the day the following morning is to make a head start - perhaps on your journey into work you can take out a pen and paper and jot down what you really need to accomplish for the day. If you have your tablet with you perhaps you can read a article or blog about the industry you work in. So your journey to work acts like a trigger to start thinking about the day ahead. Once you get into work you are already ready and raring to go.

Once you are at work why not get a cup of coffee or tea and use this as a second trigger to spend five minutes cleaning up your desk and sorting through your paper. Put away everything that isn't related to your work or tasks today. This way you only have those things on your desk that you need for the important tasks you need to achieve.

While your computer is being switched on why not take out all the relevant material for the most difficult task ahead and tackle it first thing in the morning when you have the most energy. Try and set a timer on your watch or computer to make sure you finish the task by the time you estimate.

After you have done the hardest task of the day why not spend some time catching up with your emails but put a timer on it. Say spend 30 minutes checking your emails and when you are done go for a mini break which is 10 push ups and a five minute walk around the building.

Keep each of your working sessions no longer than 90 minutes. This is so that you can keep going at a good pace because you know that a break is in sight. Once the 90 minutes are up get up and move around for five minutes, take a glass of water, have a piece of fruit or some dried nuts and then you can sit back to work again.

Lunch time, the time of the day we look most forward to, can be used effectively to relax and meet a number of our work-related goals. Why not eat out with colleagues so you can improve your networking credentials within the organization. You also can spend some of your lunch time viewing online courses in your area of expertise, you can read up on communication skills, presentation skills and any other area you feel weak in. Try and take in new bits of information about your line of work in mini-bites.

Step 1: 5 minute think the night before about work

Step 2: Wake up

Step 3: Prepare breakfast

Step 4: Have a shower

Step 5: Brush teeth

Step 6: Get dressed

Step 7: Get on public transport

Step 8: Spend 5 minutes planning your day.

Step 9: Spend 5 - 10 minute reading something about

your line of work
or work skills

Step 10: Make tea
or coffee

Step 11: 5 minutes
to clear your desk

Step 12: Start up
your computer

Step 13: 5 minutes
to take out
relevant material

Step 14: Work for
90 minutes

Step 15: Exercise
for 5 minutes

Step 16: Work for
90 minutes

Step 17: Lunch
with colleague

Step 18: Work for
90 minutes

Step 19: Exercise
for 5-10 minutes

Chapter 7. Finance Related Habit Stacking

This chapter looks at how we can use the process of habit stacking to improve our financial habits. Our finances are an area where we would all like to be wiser, savvier and successful. We would all like to earn more money, make financially sound choices and save more for tough times. We are now going to have a look at how you can use habit stacking to make more financially sound decisions and come out financially stronger.

Some Popular Financial Aims

- Educate yourself about money.

- Spend less, save more.

- Set up a strict budget to keep track of your money.

- Saving more for a rainy day.

- Know and improve your credit scores.

- Ensure a debt free life.

- Make more Money.

- Take up small side jobs.

- Building up your re fund.

- Insuring yourself.

- Giving to charity.

- Try a no spend challenge

- Downsize your life.

- Having long-term goals.

- Rewarding yourself reasonable wa

Habit Stacking as a Means to Further Your Career

Perhaps you have a couple minutes during breakfast and can use this time productively to start meeting your financial goals, why not spend five minutes reading up on the financial section of your newspaper, reading financial articles online or a financial blog to better understand how to manage your current finances. This will help you understand money and how it can be managed more effectively.

When it comes to saving money you can have a think about some of the things you can do without - perhaps the morning cup of coffee you get from Starbucks or Costa? Why not just brew your favourite brand of coffee and take it into office in a thermos flask. This act alone could save you a tidy $100-$150 which you could put away in your emergency fund each month. This act alone - brewing your own coffee - is not likely to take more than 5-7 minutes at home.

Another five minute job which will help you save at least $5-$10 on a daily basis is making your lunch at home. Why not put an apple or banana, a small packet of nuts, a homemade sandwich and a bottle of juice into your backpack. This will save you the cost of going to the deli everyday or buying an overpriced sandwich or hot dog. This again could save you between $150-$200 per month!

Perhaps on a Sunday afternoon when you are maxing out in front of the television why not pick up a pen and paper and spend five minutes budgeting. Put the income you earn each month on one side and try and put together the expenses which go out of your account each month. This might seem hard but start with the obvious expenses such as rent/mortgage, utility bills, grocery bill, clothing expenditure, entertainment and travel. Try and have a think about how much you would like to save. Put the save figure on the sheet of paper and have a think about how much you can actually spend. You can also include the amount you want to give to charity. Try and set a strict budget.

Another five minute hack you can fit into your Sunday is making a list before you go shopping. The other trick is to only buy what you put down on your list no impulsive buying. You can adopt this policy for food, clothing and electric goods. Plan before you go shopping, if you need clothes make a list of what you need, if you need electronics make a specific list of what you need.

Making Financially Sound Decisions

Step 1: Wake up

Step 2: Prepare breakfast

Step 3: Read a financial blog/article for 5 minutes

Step 4: Prepare coffee for work

Step 5: Prepare lunch for work

Step 6: Have a shower

Step 7: Brush teeth

Step 8: Get dressed

Step 9: Get on public transport

Step 10: Spend 5 minutes planning your budget

Step 9: Spend five minutes at lunch hour looking for better insurance deals

Step 10: Spending five minutes in the evening jotting down what you should buy.

Chapter 8. Developing Leisure Activities through Habit Stacking

This chapter deals with leisure activities and how to spend a little time doing what you would absolutely love to. As is the case with most people you are busy working and manning the home front and perhaps don't get time to try out the things you think you might enjoy. We think that by adopting habit stacking you can try out a little of what you like each day or each week. It comes with trying to fit small bits of leisurely activities into your day.

There is nothing like developing or spending time indulging in pursuits or hobbies that you enjoy. These hobbies could be a number of diverse and varied things: reading, watching old movies or gardening. Your leisurely pursuit could even be setting up a spa in your home during the evening. However the one difference between leisure activities and all the other facets of your life are that in case of these activities you will need to find a slot of 15-30 minutes.

Some Popular Leisurely Activities

Some of the activities we are going to list and mention in this section are:

- Reading.

- Writing.

- Watching movies.

- Artistic pursuits i.e. painting, sculpturing, woodwork, knitting, sewing, crocheting.

- Listening to/playing music.

- Cooking/baking.

- Playing sports.

- Spending time with family and friends.

- Educating yourself.

- Personal grooming/beauty treatments.

Leisurely Activities Through Habit Stacking

The starting point for developing leisurely activities is making a list of the top three to five leisure activities you would like to pursue on a daily or weekly basis. Next you need to think which activities you can do on a daily basis and which you can do on a weekly basis or after two to three days. Once again, a lot of people don't try new things as they fear they don't have adequate time however everyone you can block out 15 minutes for a number of pursuits.

Say you are looking to increase the number of books you read in a year. But you are sort of at a loose end in terms of how to fit in that reading. Well the simple solution is to schedule it in like you schedule in everything in your life. Say you want to read more you can schedule in reading for 15 minutes before going to bed or during the half an hour train journey to work.

Perhaps you wan to learn a language, you can take some audio based courses and listen to them on your travel into work. Perhaps you want to take an online learning course, maybe you can fit it into your lunch hour at your desk. The important thing to remember is to try and figure out where you have pockets of time which you don't use productively.

You love listening to music as it relaxes you, unwinds you after a long day and even helps you concentrate during work. You can listen to music as you cook and clean around the house, you can listen to music on your phone on the travel to work. In some cases you can even listen to music while working.

You enjoy cooking and baking but feel its far to time consuming and can't really manage it on a daily basis but what if we said that you can. The wonderful think about cooking is that you can multitask while cooking. You can listen to the music you want, you can listen to that language tape that you wanted to or even listen to an audio book. You can do two things at once to save time.

Do you feel run down and a tad rough on the edges and wished that you had the time and energy to do a spot of personal grooming or indulging in some beauty treatments? Well why not schedule 15 minute beauty treatments on a daily basis for yourself? Why not try one beauty treatment a day for yourself. Have a 15 minute facial one day, try a 15 minute manicure another day and a 15 minute pedicure on the third day to keep you feeling pampered and looking great.

Spending time with family and friends might not be a fifteen minute affair but perhaps you could schedule in a once a week dinner with your parents and siblings and a once a week meet up with your friends. Perhaps making these meet ups a fixed part of your week will help.

Chapter 9. Family and Relationship Habit Stacking

Nurturing good relationships with family members, friends and work colleagues take time and effort. Most of us probably feel we are at the short end of the stick when we look at personal relationships. We find ourselves engrossed in our work, busy with the technology around us and generally short of time. However, using habit stacking we can allow ourselves to keep in touch with our family and friends despite our crazy busy lives.

Whether it's phoning your parents, sending out emails to family and friends, sending out Christmas or Easter cards to your loved ones all of this takes time and organization and sometimes we tend to go really wrong in our personal relationships. It might feel that we are failing or lagging behind in the personal aspect of our life. We hope by taking these micro steps we can motivate you to help build, nurture and sustain your personal relationships.

Some Popular Personal Aims

- Keep in touch with your parents.

- Stay connected to siblings.

- Find time for friends.

- Find time to connect with work colleagues.

- Find time to connect with your local community.

- Find time to meet new people.

- Be present for your family when help is needed.

- Share a meal with your family once a week.

- Spend more time with your partner.

- Set aside some time to be with your partner/family.

- Find time to have person to person contact with family & friends.

- Find time to write letters and cards.

Habit Stacking To Turn around Your Personal Life

While one of your main aims in life might be to keep your personal relationships blossoming you might struggle to find the time or means to figure out how to do this. You might think you need hours and hours to sort out personal relationships and you won't necessarily be wrong. However, you can start off by spending small but regular amounts of time communicating with family members. It's all about seamlessly adding in new habits to your daily routine.

Say you want to stay in touch with your mum and dad on a regular basis. Why not give them a call on your way to work on a bus or train? You can give them a five minute call on a daily basis as you walk to your station. If it's a sibling you feel you haven't been giving much time to why not give them a five minute call at lunch time. If it's a friend you haven't been in touch with for some time then pop them an email asking about how they are and whether they fancy a meet. If you want to keep in touch with family and friends and add in a personalized touch why not write them a hand written note about how you miss them or would like to see them.

Although some of us might look down upon emails, texts and WhatsApp and consider them as not being real contact in this day and age they work wonderfully in helping us keep in touch with family and friends who we are separated from in distance and time. Why not spend 5-10 minutes at the end of each evening sending out a hello or hi to family members and friends you opt not to ring or get in touch with.

Connecting With Family and Friends Through Habit Stacking?

Step 1: Wake up

Step 2: Prepare breakfast

Step 3: Prepare lunch for work

Step 4: Have a shower

Step 5: Brush teeth

Step 6: Get dressed

Step 7: Leave home for work

Step 8: Call mum/dad

Step 9: Arrive at work start working

Step 10: Lunch time

Step 9: Spend five minutes calling sibling/friend.

Step 10: Spend five minutes sending a reminder to a work colleague about meeting up for coffee lunch

Step 11: Leaving work for home

Step 12: Call a friend and tell them how you miss them or want to meet up.

Step 13: Arrive home and have dinner

Step 14: Spend 5-10 minutes emailing or messaging friends and family members

Chapter 10. De-cluttering and Organizing Your Life

Another common aim we may all have but may not get very far in terms of achieving on a day-to-day basis is to have neat, clean and tidy homes, work spaces and lives. Now neat, clean and tidy may mean different things to different people but we think most people would like to have an organize and decluttered home and work space. This covers two domains of people's lives the physical domain, the mental domain and the emotional domain. You might just get exhausted thinking about these two domains; however, once again, we think small steps will go a long way in setting up the new lifestyle that you crave. If you adopt our small step by step plan you could quite easily end up with the pristine life you always wanted.

Common Decluttering and Organizing Aims

Living Space Organization

- A decluttered living space

- A tidy living space

- A clean living space

- An environmentally friendly living space

- A living space that promotes recycling

- A living space providing a peace of mind and beauty

- A living space reflecting your style

Work Space Orgaisation

- A decluttered work space

- A tidy work space

- A clean work space

- A professional looking work space

- A work space that is calming

- A work space organized for the day ahead

- A work space reflecting your style

Organized and Decluttered Living Space

You might think that you will never truly be able to declutter and organize your home but nothing could be further from this belief. We can show you how even in your morning routine you can leave a home tidier, organized and more welcoming to come home to each evening. When you get up in the morning, once you are done with your mediation, yoga, drinking glasses of water and having a think about the day why not just make your bed. There is no better way to start your day than by making your bed. Then take out your work clothes and lay them on the bed all ready to put on. Next take a quick look around your bedroom to see if there is anything which shouldn't be there - dirty clothes, coffee cups, glasses of water or anything else and remove it. You have just tidied up our bedroom and made a good start to the day.

When you head down to the kitchen to prepare breakfast and lunch for the day ahead make sure that you clean up as you go along. So any dirty cups, plates, glasses and cutlery should go back into the sink or dishwasher. Food which needs to go back into the fridge should do so, anything which needs to be thrown out should be thrown out. Kitchen surfaces should be given a quick wipe. There you have already managed to do away with the mess in the kitchen.

When you head to the bathroom for a shower and change of clothes remember to tidy up the bathroom. So, after a shower remember to rinse the shower cubicle and wipe the tiles clean or simply use a wiper. If you have shaved and brushed your teeth then give the wash basin a quick rinse and wipe. Make sure your towel is back on the towel rack and any dirty clothes in the laundry basket. You have just left your bathroom in a presentable state.

When you head out of the house and off to work why not empty the kitchen and living room waste paper baskets. This way when you get home you will have another chore ticked off your list. It's important to make sure that you choose 6 or 7 essential chores to start off with initially. This will make it seem manageable and a part of your daily routine.

Step 1: Wake Up

Step 2: Drink water

Step 3: Five minutes of exercise

Step 4: Take your vitamin

Step 5: Make your bed

Step 6: Lay out your clothes

Step 7: Remove anything not part of your bedroom

Step 8: Eat a fruit

Step 9:Prepare a healthy breakfast

Step 10: Load up the dishwasher

Step 11: Wipe the kitchen surfaces

Step 12: Have a shower

Step 13: Wipe down the shower cubicle

Step 14: Brush your teeth

Step 15: Floss your teeth

Step 16: Rinse and wipe down the washbasin

Step 17: Hang your towel and put dirty clothes and laundry basket

Step 18: Heading off to work

Organized and Decluttered Work Space

An organized and decluttered work space will allow you to be more productive, creative and generally efficient all around. However, if truth be told most of us have a work station or work desk that looks like a pig sty. This generally adds to our confusion, mess and slows down all the vital tasks we do during the day. However, with just a little practice and five or six simple tasks we can clear up this mess in no time at all.

We start with the evening around about the time we leave for home - why not spent 5-10 minutes tidying up the day's mess at your work table before leaving. Any glasses, cups, plates, cutlery can be taken back to the cafeteria, uneaten food can be thrown away, completed paper work can be filed away. Post-it notes pertaining to that day's deadlines thrown out. Try and leave the desk as neat and tidy as you can for the new day ahead.

When you reach home always check your electronic calendar for the next day and plan ahead. Is there anything you can spend a few minutes thinking about or doing which will help the next day go smoother for you. If there is something which needs to be thought out or planned for the day ahead then take out five to ten minutes at home and carry it out.

When you arrive at work and while you are putting your bag down and getting a cup of tea/coffee ready spend five minutes clearing your desk of all the things you don't need. While your computer is starting up and you are waiting to log in take out the things you need.

Once your computer is on check your electronic calendar and desk organizer to have a look at what work you will be doing today. Before you start work, sit down with a notepad and pen and prioritize the top five things you need to do. Now you are ready to start your day!

Other tips that you can incorporate into your day are: putting away any files or papers once work on a particular project is complete. Only checking emails at certain times of the day so that you aren't distracted and your emails don't serve as a distraction. Remember to keep some disinfectant wet wipes or spray and a dusting cloth at your desk so that you can wipe your desk once you have finished a snack or meal.

All of these small actions will help make a big difference to making your work place organized, tidy and generally clean. It will give you the clean slate start that you crave at the beginning of each day.

Step 1: Start the evening before and tidy up your desk before leaving.

Step 2: Before going to bed organize your electronic calendar or the day ahead.

Step 3: Make a cup of tea when you arrive at work.

Step 4: Clear desk of all things you won't tackle today.

Step 5: Start up your computer.

Step 6: Only take out things you will be

working on in the morning.

Step 7: Check your electronic calendar and desk organizer.

Step 8: Before starting work spend five minutes shredding all paper you don't need.

Step 9: Spend 5-10 minutes on any administrative tasks you need to deal with.

Step 10: Every time you finish working on a project put away the paper work or material.

Step 11: Every time you finish working on a project spend 5-10 minutes checking up on your emails and then shut the browser.

Step 12: Keep all internet windows shut while corresponding or writing on your computer.

Chapter 11. Spiritual Habit Stacking

This chapter is for those of you who would like to infuse a bit of spirituality into your day-to-day life. We often find ourselves yearning for something less to do with the physical aspects or the material things in life. We often find ourselves doing soul searching and doing some introspection and realizing that we are looking for something purer, simpler, and soulful in our lives. For those of you who realize that you are craving to look into your spiritual needs and nourish them we give you habit stacking as the solution.

Being spiritual can mean many different, wonderful and genuine things to many people. You might find spirituality in the form of a formal faith or religion. You might already be part of a faith which you haven't found much time for and perhaps want to turn your attention to it. You might not be part of any organized faith but you know you want to be in touch with your spirituality. Or perhaps you don't know what spirituality is but you are looking to get in touch with your inner self - that is also a form of spirituality.

Whatever your inclination in terms of spirituality this chapter will help you realize that you can get in touch with your inner spirituality on a daily basis in small manageable portions. Some common spiritual aims which many of you might want yourself craving for are:

- Finding time for yourself.

- Finding time to write down what you want out of life.

- Walking up to a spiritual ritual.

- Practicing meditation.

- Practicing gentle exercise.

- Being at one with nature.

- Having a spiritual experience with your family.

- Having a spiritual moment with your pet.

- Having a spiritual tea or coffee drinking moment.

- Carrying an act of kindness.

- Finding time throughout the day to have some spiritual time for yourself.

- Ending your day
  on a spiritual note.

Bringing Spirituality into Your Life With Habit Stacking

Now you don't have to turn into a recluse, a Sufi or a mystic to bring spirituality into your daily life. However, you do need some time to yourself on a daily basis in order to get in touch with your inner self. Now it might not be a lot of time that you need, but you need to be consistent in your attention to yourself and your spiritual needs.

You can start your day with a number of spiritual acts as a couple of minutes of meditation, saying a prayer or chant, writing in your journal. Perhaps you want to potter around your garden or just water your house plants to find a balance with nature. You could feel spiritual simply by showering love and attention on your pet.

There are other ways to sneak in some spirituality into your day, you could meditate or have a reflection session as you make your tea or brew your coffee. You could set your intention for the day before leaving home for work. You could leave home after having a moment of peace and

Step 1: Wake up half an hour earlier.

Step 2: Practice five minutes of meditation.

Step 3: Say a prayer, a chant, or a positive mantra.

Step 4: Spend five minutes writing in your journal about your spiritual needs.

Step 5: Get up and water plants in your home.

Step 6: Hug your pet and spend 5-10 minutes with them.

Step 7:Prepare a healthy breakfast.

Step 8: Have a five minute tea/coffee brewing ritual.

Step 9: Have a shower.

Step 10: Brush and floss your teeth.

Step 11: Get dressed.

Step 12: Put on some moisturizer.

Step 13: Get ready for the day ahead by setting your intention for the day.

Step 14: Leave home

with a clear head and a
positive   self.

PART III: SMALL TIPS TO IMPROVE YOUR LIFE AND MAKE IT BETTER

Chapter 12. 11 Small Tips to Make you Life Better

This final chapter will provide you with encouragement to start a 30-day challenge of habit stacking. While we all know what is good for us sometimes we just don't do what is required from us. We seem to be stuck in a rut, just have a bad case of inertia, or are scared to try something new for the fear of failing badly. We have some tips to help you reduce some of the resistance you might have to change.

1. **No time like the present:** Why not start immediately by getting a pen and paper and writing down some positive habits you would like to inculcate in your daily routine. Keep your list to a minimum of three and maximum of five new habits - it's better not to overdo things at an early stage.

2. **Know your daily routine:** Take another piece of paper and quickly list down your daily routine. Be prepared to spend about 15-20 minutes on this list as there are dozens of things you will be doing through out the day. Try and make this list as

detailed as possible so that it can help you with the habit stacking you are hopefully going to start tomorrow!

3. **Set up a checklist:** This might seem tedious and a bit of an overkill but believe us when we say it will help get the job done when nothing else will. Jot down on your check list what you hope to achieve at the end of each day and then make sure you run through the check list twice a day.

4. **Set your alarm clock half an hour earlier:** While you might yelp at the idea of having to get up earlier, it will help you introduce the small yet effective new steps into your daily routine. But these small steps need a little extra time to enforce and you need time to get used to them being part of your day.

5. **Start with one habit:** If you are scared you won't be able to include the five or six new habits into your new day why not start with one new habit. Why not just make this your 30 day challenge - be it five minutes of yoga each morning, meditation, writing, mindfulness, pampering yourself with a beauty

treatment, or tidying up the house. Just start somewhere so that you have made a start.

6. **Celebrate your small victories:** You need to be able to celebrate even if it's for the tiny gains you make each day. Celebrate by being good to yourself, giving yourself some time to relax, or treating yourself to your favourite song, spraying on your favourite perfume or wearing your favourite dress. If you reward yourself for your gains then you are more likely to make more bigger and better gains.

7. **Love and be kind to yourself:** When you are trying to make important changes in your life it's too easy to be hard on yourself, dislike yourself or think of yourself as unworthy of love, praise and positive attention. It's a difficult or important times in your life that you need to show some tender loving care towards yourself.

8. **About the journey as much as the goal:** It's important to realize that habit stacking will get you to the end goals but also teach your more about yourself and enrich your life with

the journey you take to get to your goal. By the time you attain some of your goals and become comfortable with your new habits you will be wiser, smarter, and savvier about yourself. You will know what makes you tick and what can hold you back.

9. **Setbacks are inevitable:** Setbacks are inevitable in life and you shouldn't fear them. Setbacks provide an important learning and self-correcting opportunity. Setbacks also teach you a thing or two about how you think and behave.

10. **Keep going:** You need to remember that it takes anywhere between 21-45 days for a new habit to take root in your daily routine. You just have to keep going, keep persevering and trying to ensure that you can plug these new habits into your day. There will come a point where they will just seamlessly become a part of your daily routine.

11. **Keep aiming high:** Finally, the important thing to remember is once you incorporate your first set of good habits into your daily routine there is no reason to stop. Why not

think about what else you would like to achieve in your life and continue on this path of improvement and self-learning.

Conclusion

I really hope that this book helped you to understand yourself and improve your life. Hope that habit stacking. I hope that the habit stacking will be the great beginning of your successful and happy life!